SUPERHEROES
OF THE BIBLE

ACTION AND ADVENTURE
STORIES ABOUT REAL-LIFE HEROES

SUPERHEROES
OF THE BIBLE

ACTION AND ADVENTURE
STORIES ABOUT REAL-LIFE HEROES

FAITH

IS THEIR SECRET WEAPON

BY *CARA STEVENS*
ILLUSTRATED BY *AMANDA BRACK*

Good Books

New York, New York

Good Books books may be purchased in bulk at special discounts for sales promotion, corporate gifts, fundraising, or educational purposes. Special editions can also be created to specifications. For details, contact the Special Sales Department, Good Books, 307 West 36th Street, 11th Floor, New York, NY 10018 or info@skyhorsepublishing.com.

Good Books is an imprint of Skyhorse Publishing, Inc.®, a Delaware corporation.

Visit our website at www.goodbooks.com.

10 9 8 7 6 5 4 3 2 1

Library of Congress Cataloging-in-Publication Data is available on file.

Print ISBN: 978-1-68099-322-6
ebook ISBN: 978-1-68099-328-8

Printed in China

CONTENTS

WHAT DOES IT TAKE TO BE A SUPERHERO FOR GOD?

All of the heroes in this book did amazing things. Think about . . .

- Joshua, who fought bravely against the great army of Jericho

- Elijah, the prophet who stood up to a powerful king and brought down fire from heaven

- David, who battled and defeated the giant, Goliath

- Esther, who boldly went to the king's palace and spoke up with a plan to save her people

- Paul, who went to prison for his faith

But aside from Jesus, these men and women weren't perfect people. So how did they get so strong and powerful? With God's help! God can work through anyone and make a superhero of faith. So as you enjoy each story, ask God to make *you* a superhero for Him!

The Story of Moses

A SERIES OF STRANGE EVENTS CREATED A HERO WHO RESCUED HIS PEOPLE FROM SLAVERY.

Moses was a miracle from the start. At the time he was born, his Israelite people were slaves to the Egyptians. The Egyptians feared their slaves might turn against them, and they feared how many Israelites were being born. So the king of Egypt, Pharaoh, ordered his people to drown all Israelite baby boys in the river.

When Moses's mother gave birth to a boy, she hid him for three months to protect him. When she couldn't hide him any longer, she placed him in a basket in the tall grass by the river. His sister watched to see what would happen.

Of all people, Pharaoh's daughter found the baby. Although she knew he wasn't

GOD KEPT MOSES SAFE FOR A BIG ADVENTURE.

Egyptian, she adopted him as her own. Thanks to his sister Miriam, Moses's own mother was hired to take care of him.

We don't know how, but as Moses grew up, he knew he was not an Egyptian. He felt connected to his true people of Israel. One day, he saw an Egyptian soldier beating a slave. Moses could not contain his anger, and he killed the soldier. When Pharaoh found out, he was very angry.

Moses ran away to a place called Midian, where he was welcomed by a priest and his daughters. Moses fell in love with one of the daughters, Zipporah, and he married her. He stayed in Midian for a long time, taking care of sheep and living a quiet life.

MOSES WANTED TO SAVE HIS PEOPLE FROM SLAVERY.

During this time, the old Pharaoh died and a new Pharaoh took his place. Still, Moses's people were kept as slaves and were treated very badly. No one knew what to do, so they prayed for answers.

MOSES HEARD GOD SPEAK FROM A BURNING BUSH!

One day, Moses was caring for his sheep when he came upon a very unusual sight. A bush was on fire. But it wasn't an ordinary fire. The bush was in flames, but the fire was not spreading. The bush wasn't turning black or becoming ashes. As he went closer to investigate, a voice from the bush called his name!

Moses knew that this voice was God.
"I am here!" he called back.
"I am sending you to free the Israelites from Pharaoh," God told him.

Moses was surprised—and afraid. He was just one ordinary man. How could he, a shepherd, challenge a mighty pharaoh and win? "I will be with you," God told him. Not only did God promise to lead Moses and guide him, but also to provide miracles to prove to the Israelites and Pharaoh that Moses had God on his side.

"Throw your shepherd's staff on the ground," God told Moses. Moses obeyed. As soon as the staff hit the earth, it transformed into a snake! Then God instructed Moses to pick

MOSES'S STAFF TURNED INTO A SNAKE!

the snake up by its tail. He did, and the snake turned back into a staff.

God told Moses that he would give him other miracles, too, but still Moses was unsure. Finally, God offered to send Moses's brother Aaron to help him. Together they would help free the slaves and lead their people to a new land. Moses and Aaron went to Pharaoh and demanded that he let the slaves go. Of course, Pharaoh said no. In fact, Pharaoh made the slaves work even harder.

But Moses and Aaron did not give up. They went back to Pharaoh. To convince Pharaoh of God's power, Aaron threw his staff on the ground just as Moses had. It turned into a snake as soon as it hit the ground. Pharaoh wasn't impressed. He brought in magicians who performed the same trick. Aaron's snake then ate the magicians' snakes, but still Pharaoh was not afraid. He sent Moses and Aaron away. He would not let the slaves go.

Again Moses and Aaron returned. Moses told Pharaoh to let their people go or he would turn the water in the river into blood. When Pharaoh said no once more, Aaron struck the water with his staff and the clear, clean water turned dark red. The fish died, and a terrible smell rose up from the river. Still Pharaoh stood his ground, because his magicians did the same with their tricks. He sent Moses and Aaron away.

One week later, God told Moses to return to Pharaoh to see if he would change his mind. When Pharaoh still refused, Moses told him that worse things were coming. He would bring a plague of frogs upon the land.

Sure enough, when Pharaoh once again said no, Aaron raised his hand over the waters and frogs covered the land. There were frogs in the kitchens and frogs on the floor, frogs on the beds and frogs on their heads. Again, Pharaoh's magicians performed a trick of their own to call more frogs. What now?

Pharaoh called Moses and Aaron before him. "Please pray to the Lord to make it stop! Make the frogs go away and I'll let your people go!" Moses

MOSES USED A STORM OF BUGS AGAINST PHARAOH.

through Moses and Aaron. All the bugs on the ground and in the air swarmed and made the Egyptians sick and uncomfortable. And this time, Pharaoh's magicians couldn't make their tricks work. Again, Pharaoh agreed to set the slaves free but then changed his mind.

Next, all of the Egyptians' working animals and pets died while the Israelites' animals stayed healthy. Then Moses tossed soot from a fireplace into the air and when it came down, the skin of every Egyptian was covered with sores. A hailstorm

did as Pharaoh asked, but once the frogs were gone, Pharaoh changed his mind.

Day after day, God sent plagues upon the Egyptians

MOSES DIDN'T GIVE UP ON FREEING HIS PEOPLE!

followed that killed everything in its path, sparing only the land where the Israelites lived.

Would all this trouble work to set the slaves free? Once again, Pharaoh sent for Moses and Aaron and agreed to release the slaves. Moses stopped the storm, only to have Pharaoh change his mind again.

But Pharaoh's answer was never accepted as final. God told Moses to raise his arms to the heavens and He sent a storm of locusts—big, green bugs that ate all the crops and the food they had stored. Pharaoh cried, "Enough! Make it stop! I will do what you ask!" Moses prayed to God to send a wind to blow all the locusts into the sea.

As expected, Pharaoh changed his mind. In response, God sent a great darkness over the land—except where the people of Israel lived. The sun didn't shine, and neither did the stars or the moon. No fire or even the glow of a firefly broke through the darkness. The Egyptians could not move or see. The people were starving and thirsty and hurt because

of the other plagues God had already brought upon the land.

Finally, Pharaoh told Moses he would let his people go, but that they would need to leave their animals behind. Moses did not agree, and Pharaoh would not give in. Instead, he told Moses to go and never come back.

But God had something different in mind. He told Moses there was one more plague to come. Every oldest son in Egypt would die, but the Israelites would be protected if they followed God's instructions to mark their homes in a special way.

Moses sent messengers through the Israelite camps to spread the message to their people. He told every Israelite family to place lamb's blood on the doorpost of each house. This way, when the plague was sent down from the heavens, only the houses without lamb's blood at the door would get touched. The Israelite children would be saved, or passed over, so this miracle is called Passover.

That night, as the Israelites feasted on the meat from the lambs, the plague struck the

Egyptian families. The oldest child of every Egyptian family died, including Pharaoh's son. Pharaoh was afraid everyone would die if he didn't agree to let the slaves go free. He called for Moses and Aaron and demanded that they take their families and leave immediately.

Moses knew they didn't have much time to gather their belongings and leave. The Pharaoh had changed his mind many times already! Moses, his brother Aaron, and his sister Miriam gathered the people together and led them out of Egypt as quickly as possible.

By day, God led them in a cloud; by night, he led them with fire. But God warned Moses that they hadn't seen the last of the Egyptians.

Sure enough, as soon as the Israelites had left, Pharaoh changed his mind once again. He took his soldiers and 600 chariots after the Israelites to bring them back as slaves.

Fortunately, Moses and his people had made a good head start. They traveled as far as the banks of the Red Sea. But they had no boats and no way to cross the river! With the Egyptian army approaching and no escape, the Israelites were terrified.

Moses knew God would provide a way. God told him to raise his staff in the air and stretch his hand out over the sea. A super-strong wind blew the water all night until it separated the waters of the sea into two walls with a muddy crossing down the middle. The Israelites were able to move quickly across the sea.

When the Egyptians tried to follow them, their chariots got stuck. Moses reached out his hand and the walls of water came crashing back down. Not one of the Egyptians survived.

On the opposite bank of the Red Sea, Moses's sister Miriam led the people with song and dance. They were grateful to finally be free, thanks to Moses's trust in the power of God and His promises.

But there's more to the story: the Israelites wandered in the desert for the next forty years. Some people lost hope after just days. There was no water or food. But whenever

Thou shalt have no other gods before me
Thou shalt not make unto thee any graven image
Thou shalt not take the name of the lord thy God in vain
Remember the Sabbath day, to keep it holy
Honor thy father and thy mother
Thou shalt not kill
Thou shalt not commit adultery
Thou shalt not steal
Thou shalt not bear false witness
Thou shalt not covet

MOSES WAS GOD'S MESSENGER TO DELIVER THE TEN COMMANDMENTS.

forgot the miracles that God provided through Moses.

God saw what was happening. He called Moses to the top of a mountain and gave him the Ten Commandments—a set of laws designed to protect His people. Moses was gone for a long time. The people waited for him at the foot of the mountain, but soon they grew restless for a leader.

Aaron told them to bring all their gold and jewels to him. He made the treasures into a metal statue of a god that looked like a calf. They celebrated and worshipped the new god.

When Moses came back down with the Ten Commandments written in stone, he was so angry at Aaron and his people that he threw down the stone tablets and they shattered. He pushed the golden calf into the fire and it melted. Moses went back up the mountain, where God provided new tablets. When

they needed help, Moses simply turned to God. God led Moses to a stick that when placed in bad water made it drinkable. God also led the people to water in other places as they traveled through the desert.

For food, God covered the land with quail in the evening and sent bread like frost on the ground in the morning. They called the bread *manna*. Still, some people lost faith and he came back, his face was shining because he had spoken with God.

Although he was at first afraid of all God asked him to do, Moses never gave up on God or his people. Moses led his people for forty years in the desert before they were able to enter the land God had promised them when He set them free from Pharaoh. Thanks to Moses, the Israelites were free and had a strong faith that would carry them through troubled times—long after Moses died at the age of 120.

Where in the Bible?

You can read about Moses in Exodus, Leviticus, Numbers, and Deuteronomy. He's also mentioned in Acts 7:20–44 and Hebrews 11:23–29. Some of the highlights:

- Moses's birth and travel to the palace: Exodus 1–2

- Moses and the burning bush: Exodus 3–4

- Moses and the plagues: Exodus 7–11

- The First Passover: Exodus 12

- The Israelites walk across the sea: Exodus 13:17–14:31

Pray to Be . . . Super-Trusting in God

The miracles that Moses showed were amazing, but their power came from God. When he was in trouble or doubting, Moses turned to God for the answers. And he remembered to give Him the glory. That's what made Moses a superhero of faith.

- Thank God for how He provides miracles and keeps His promises.

- Pray to God for help when something seems impossible.

- Listen to God when He says not to be afraid.

THE STORY OF MIRIAM

A SMALL GIRL TOOK A BOLD STEP AND GAVE AN IMPORTANT GIFT TO HER PEOPLE.

Even superheroes of faith were once babies. Moses, the hero who rescued his people from slavery and parted the Red Sea, was no exception. When Moses was a small, helpless baby, his parents were afraid he would be killed.

But God had a plan to use a young girl to save his life. His sister Miriam watched over baby Moses to make sure he would be okay.

Why was baby Moses in danger? He was born in a time when Israelites were strong and growing in numbers. The leader of Egypt, Pharaoh, worried that the Israelites would take over. He used his power to make all the Israelites his slaves.

Under his rule, the Israelites had no rights at all. They worked from morning to night in the hot desert sun, with taskmasters whipping their backs if they didn't work hard or fast enough.

Despite how badly they were treated, the Israelites stayed strong and their numbers grew even greater.

This turn of events made Pharaoh really angry. He ordered his soldiers to kill the sons of every slave as soon as they were born. Many people tried to hide their babies to keep them safe, but as soon as the soldiers heard the cries, they carried out Pharaoh's orders.

So Miriam's parents were very worried when her baby brother was born. They hid their baby for a little while, but after three months, the soldiers came poking around. Miriam's parents grew very afraid. They could no longer hide their son's strong cries. They placed him in a basket by the river, where they hoped he would be safer.

Miriam hid in the tall grass and watched her baby brother. Her heart was breaking to see

MIRIAM WANTED TO PROTECT HER BABY BROTHER.

PHARAOH'S DAUGHTER FINDING MOSES WAS PART OF GOD'S PLAN.

him go. She knew there were great things in store for this baby. As Miriam watched from the tall grass, she saw a young woman walking toward the water. Miriam could tell she was part of the Pharaoh's family because she was dressed in fine robes and jewels.

As the young woman reached the water, she let out a happy cry: "It's a baby in a basket!" She looked lovingly at the baby. She knew the baby must have come from the slave village, but she didn't care. She took one look at him and decided he would be hers from that day on.

All this time, Miriam had been watching from her hiding spot. When she saw how much love and care the woman showed for her little brother, Miriam boldly came forward. She felt that God somehow wanted her to step in. So she quickly offered to find a woman from the slave village to feed and care for the baby so the Pharaoh's daughter could raise him as her own son. The woman agreed, and Miriam went

off at once to tell her mother the good news. And that is how Moses came to be raised in the Pharaoh's home and to be cared for by his own mother.

Because of Miriam, Moses went on to save his people and release them from slavery. But while Moses lived in the palace, Miriam went back to her village and grew up as a slave.

Her sacrifice and heroism did not go unnoticed. When Moses grew up and one day led the Israelites across the Red Sea, drowning their enemies who

MIRIAM'S COURAGE BROUGHT MOSES BACK TO HIS MOTHER!

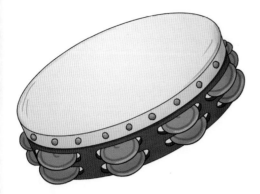

followed after them, he had his sister Miriam by his side.

When the Israelites fled Egypt, they had just a few moments to grab only the most necessary things from their homes. They didn't even have time for their bread dough to rise.

The women packed their few prized possessions as quickly as they could. They had to leave before Pharaoh changed his mind and sent his soldiers after them. But some, like Miriam, were filled with so much hope that they packed their tambourines and musical instruments as well.

And so it was that the Israelites crossed the Red Sea to safety. The enemy soldiers followed after them but drowned as the water covered their tracks. The people let out a cry of relief, and Miriam led them with a beautiful song and dance. She played her tambourine, and one by one the women and men followed along, playing their instruments and celebrating.

MIRIAM OBEYED, AND HER PEOPLE WERE REWARDED!

MIRIAM'S GIFT OF MUSIC
FILLED HER PEOPLE WITH HOPE !

The song Miriam sang was so lovely and so memorable that it is still remembered today, thousands of years later. When her job of looking after her baby brother was complete, Miriam helped lead her people in the desert and give them hope when all hope was lost.

Where in the Bible?

You can read about Miriam in Exodus and Numbers. Some of the highlights:

- Miriam with baby Moses: Exodus 2:7–8
- Miriam celebrates after crossing the Red Sea: Exodus 15:20

Pray to Be . . . Super-Seeing

Miriam watched for a chance to help Moses, and she grabbed it when she saw it. Because of the courage she had to approach Pharaoh's daughter, Moses and her people were rescued.

- Thank God for how He protects us.

- Pray to God to show you ways to help others.

- Listen to God when He says you are important to His work.

The Story of Joshua

FLOODWATERS AND THICK WALLS COULDN'T STOP THIS GREAT LEADER WITH GOD ON HIS SIDE.

The Israelites spent four hundred years as slaves. So just imagine how excited they were to finally come near the land God promised them. But when they got close to the land of Canaan, there was just one sort of big problem. People were already living there. What to do?

THE PROMISED LAND WAS FILLED WITH GOOD THINGS!

God gave Moses a plan. He sent twelve spies to find out what the land was like and see if it was possible for them to go in and take over. When the spies returned, ten of them agreed on how they saw the land.

The good news: they said the land was beautiful and fruitful, and showed the fresh fruits they had brought back. The bad news, according to their report: the cities were well guarded and strong. The people were powerful, some even giants. The spies felt they could never win in an invasion.

What about the other two spies? Joshua and Caleb brought back a different report. Their faith in God and His gift of the Promised Land was so strong that they were determined to find a way to take the land as their own. Caleb encouraged the others, "We can certainly do it."

JOSHUA OBEYED GOD, AND THE WATERS STOPPED FLOWING!

Together, Joshua and Caleb reminded the people,

"Do not be afraid of the people of the land, because we will swallow them up . . . the Lord is with us."

But instead of listening, the people actually threatened to stone them. God came to Joshua and Caleb's rescue. The spies who had brought back the bad report and spread grumbling among the people were struck down and died of a plague. The people were then made to wander in the desert for forty years for their lack of faith.

When the people approached the Promised Land a second time, Moses was growing old. God told Moses to give power to a new leader. That leader was Joshua. His courage and faith in God's promises stood out.

Joshua's first task was to lead the people across the Jordan River according to God's command. At this time of year, the river would be at flood stage. But God told Joshua not to be afraid. Joshua listened and obeyed what God had told him to do.

The priests went first. As soon as their feet touched the water, the water stopped flowing. The priests were to stay in the river until all the people were able to cross on dry ground. That's exactly what happened. As soon as the priests stepped out of the river area, the waters began to rush again.

In the meantime, Joshua had already begun to deal with the next challenge. He sent spies ahead to check out the land, especially the city of Jericho. The spies reported that the people of Jericho were afraid of

WITH GOD ON HIS SIDE, JOSHUA HAD MORE POWER THAN ALL THE ARMIES COMBINED.

JERICHO'S WALLS—UP TO TWENTY-FIVE FEET
HIGH AND TWENTY FEET THICK—TUMBLED DOWN!

them. That was a good start. But Joshua knew that the Israelites weren't as strong as their opponents. They didn't have a lot of weapons or a high-walled city like Jericho to hide behind. What now?

Just in time, an angel appeared and God spoke to Joshua. God said that Jericho would fall to the Israelites. All Joshua needed to do was follow an unusual plan. The Israelites first marched around the walls of the city once every day for six days, with the priests leading the march.

On the seventh day, they marched around the walls seven times while the priests blew their

HORNS BECAME POWERFUL AGAINST THE ENEMY!

horns. With one last great blow of the priests' horns, the people joined in with shouts and the walls of Jericho came tumbling down, leaving the city with no defenses.

Word spread across the land that Joshua's small army had defeated the powerful city of Jericho, armed only with a loud cry. The kings of neighboring lands grew afraid. They gathered together and decided to unite to attack the Israelites.

Joshua led his people into battle. It was one army against several. They were clearly outnumbered. But with God on his side, Joshua had more power than all the armies combined. First, God brought down hail on his enemies to block their path. The Israelites were winning against the enemies they were facing, but more armies were on the way.

There wasn't enough time to face off against every troop before nightfall. If they had to stop fighting when it grew dark, by the time the sun came up, the other armies would have had time to band together and overpower them. What Joshua needed was for time to stop. He needed more daylight to get the job done.

JOSHUA BOLDLY ASKED GOD TO MAKE THE SUN AND MOON STAND STILL.

IT WAS THE LONGEST DAY EVER!

the end of the longest day ever, the Israelites had won.

Joshua went on to lead his people through more battles. He eventually won the land that God had promised long, long ago.

Where in the Bible?

You can read all about Joshua in Exodus, Numbers, Deuteronomy, and Joshua. Some of the highlights:

- Spies check out Canaan: Numbers 13, 14:26–38

- Joshua becomes leader: Number 27:15–23

- Crossing the Jordan River: Joshua 3–4:18

- The Battle of Jericho: Joshua 5:13–6:20

- The longest day ever: Joshua 10:12–14

So Joshua called out to God for the sun and the moon to stand still. For a full day, the sun was out and the Israelites fought their enemies as they arrived. The enemies did not have time to work together and craft a battle plan. They were too busy fighting Joshua and his army. At

Pray to Be . . . Super-Obedient to God

Joshua was a great leader because he followed God—even when the commands seemed strange. He relied on his faith, not force, to give him power.

- Thank God for always wanting the best for us.

- Pray to God for answers when you don't know how to get out of a situation.

- Listen to God's ways to get to good places.

THE STORY OF DEBORAH AND JAEL

MEET TWO HEROINES WHO LISTENED TO GOD AND STEPPED OUT IN FAITH TO BRING PEACE TO THE LAND.

Before the people of Israel were united under King Saul and King David, the twelve tribes of Israel were ruled separately. Each tribe had judges to help lead the people and keep them on the right path. But the judges couldn't always keep their people from turning away from the commandments and getting into trouble.

When the people fell on hard times, they cried out to God for help, and God would send leaders in the form of judges and prophets. One of the judges was named Deborah. She not only had the power to lead the people, but she was a prophetess. A prophetess had the special gift of knowing God's plans and warning the people to follow.

Every day, Deborah would sit on a hill under a palm tree, and people would come to her with questions. She would help them sort out their problems and look for what God wanted to happen in their lives.

During that time, King Jabin of Hazor was a Canaanite who was very cruel to the Israelites. His general, Sisera, carried out the king's orders with no mercy. The people came to Deborah for

DEBORAH HAD THE SUPERPOWER OF KNOWING WHAT GOD WANTED TO HAPPEN.

GOD HELPED BARAK'S ARMY EASILY
BEAT SISERA'S ARMY!

be important to rally his troops and give them courage.

Barak gathered ten thousand men, as Deborah commanded. Then he and Deborah left the city walls to find Sisera and his men to fight. But how would they go against Sisera's army of horse-drawn chariots? At Deborah's command, they lured Sisera's army to them to fight. Just as Sisera's chariots approached, God sent crazy rain and hail, causing flooding and trouble for the chariots.

help. Her gift of knowing God's will was valued. She knew to send for a man named Barak to lead her people's army and beat Sisera.

Barak had one condition: Deborah had to join them in battle. Deborah agreed, but she cautioned him that it would come at a cost. If she went with Barak into battle, they would win, but a woman would get credit for it, not him. Barak went along with that plan, knowing that having Deborah there would

As Sisera's men abandoned their chariots and lost their swords in the confusion, the Israelites had the advantage. They easily defeated Sisera's armies. Sisera fled the scene to regroup and figure out his next move. He had more armies at his command, but he needed time to gather them and plan his next battle.

Sisera found shelter in the tent of Jael, the wife of a man named Heber the Kenite. It

JAEL'S PLAN STARTED WITH A CUP OF MILK.

seemed to be a perfect hideout. Heber was known to be friendly with King Jabin, plus no one would expect to find Sisera in a woman's tent.

Unfortunately for Sisera, Jael was not a fan of Sisera or King Jabin. On the front lines of the war, she had seen how badly Sisera treated the Israelites. When Sisera arrived at her tent, she seized her opportunity to be a heroine. She knew she had one chance to make sure no more innocent people would die at Sisera's hands.

Jael pretended to be a gracious hostess. She invited him to lie down and she covered him with a blanket. She served him warm milk with herbs to help him rest. When Jael was certain Sisera was fast asleep, she looked around for a weapon and realized she didn't have one!

She couldn't risk leaving and waking Sisera up, so she searched frantically around the tent. Her eyes lit on a tent stake in the corner. It was used to secure the tent in the ground and keep it from blowing away even in harsh weather. It wasn't a sword or a knife, but it was sturdy and sharp, and it would have to do.

Quickly and quietly Jael approached the sleeping general. She raised the tent stake and, with one swift movement, brought it down on Sisera's head, killing him in his sleep.

Just then, she heard someone approaching the tent. Was it someone who would be angry with her and punish her? she wondered. Whether it was friend or foe, she decided she was not going to run and hide. She bravely went out to meet the person at the entrance of the tent, ready to face the consequences. Fortunately, it was Barak, the commander of the Israelites! She brought

SISERA THOUGHT HE HAD FOUND THE PERFECT HIDEOUT.

him in and showed him the slain Sisera. Barak was very grateful to Jael. He realized that Deborah had seen God's hand in the plan.

The Canaanites were defeated, and for the next forty years Deborah ruled in peace, thanks to Jael's bravery. Deborah even wrote a song commemorating the acts of Jael, the everyday heroine who saved the people and brought peace to the land.

Where in the Bible?

You can read about Deborah and Jael in Judges. Some of the highlights:

- Deborah calls upon Barak: Judges 4:1–16

- Jael delivers the Israelites from Sisera: Judges 4:17–24

- The song of Deborah: Judges 5

Pray to Be . . . Super-Wise in God's Ways

Deborah had the special gift of knowing God's ways. But she didn't just keep the information to herself; she acted on her wisdom to inspire and help her people. Jael saw through cruel Sisera and sided with God's people, even though King Jabin's side looked like it would win.

- Thank God for the wisdom He gives you.

- Pray to God to know Him even better.

- Listen to and learn from others who know God well.

The Story of Samson

GOD HAD BIG PLANS FOR THIS MIGHTY STRONGMAN—NO MATTER WHAT MISTAKES HE MADE ALONG THE WAY.

For many years, the people of Israel lived peacefully in Palestine. But then the Philistines gained control. They were not very kind to the Israelites, and God saw the suffering. He sent an angel down to earth with a message of hope for His people.

SAMSON WAS A GIFT FROM GOD.

The angel appeared to an Israelite woman who had not been able to have children, and told her that she would soon have a son. This son would be blessed by God in a special way as he grew up. Through him, God would begin to rescue the Israelites from the harsh rule of the Philistines.

But in return, this son must dedicate his life to God. As a sign of that promise, he must never cut his hair, never drink wine or even eat grapes, and never go near anything dead.

He must follow this strange but special path God set for him.

The boy was born, just as the angel said. He was named Samson. As he grew up, he obeyed God's special rules for him, such as never cutting his hair. He was blessed and grew very strong with God.

While Samson's body was strong, his self-control was not. Samson was quick to fall in love, and he was also quick to anger. That combination got him into quite a few bad situations. But the Lord had a plan for him, and Samson had faith that God would guide him to carry out his purpose.

When Samson was old enough to marry, he met a beautiful Philistine woman from the nearby village of Timnah.

He decided that she was the one woman in all the world who would make him happy. His parents did not approve of his marrying an enemy, but Samson would not listen to their pleas. He was determined to marry her.

What happened? Eventually, Samson's parents agreed to meet the girl and her family. They left their home and started to walk to Timnah. Samson was so excited, he ran ahead. All alone in the middle of a vineyard, he was surprised by a great roaring lion! As the lion sprang up toward him, Samson felt the Spirit of the Lord fill him.

Samson gathered all the strength he had been given, grabbed the charging lion, and tore it apart with his bare hands! Samson was amazed at his own strength, but he was ashamed that he had killed one of God's creatures. Instead of going home to clean himself and ask God's forgiveness, he rejoined his parents on the walk and did not tell them what had happened in the vineyard.

Some time later, as Samson walked once again to Timnah, he

SAMSON FOUGHT A LION WITH HIS BARE HANDS!

went by the vineyard where he had killed the lion. When he saw the lion's body, he discovered a very strange thing. A swarm of bees had made a nest in the lion's body, and it was filled with honey!

Although Samson knew it was wrong to touch the dead animal, he couldn't resist the sweet, delicious honey. He scooped it up and licked his fingers clean, not even noticing the angry bees swarming around him, warning him away. He was the mighty Samson, after all. A few little bees couldn't hurt such a blessed, strong man of God! He kept the lion a secret, and he even gave some of the forbidden honey to his parents.

Finally, Samson's parents agreed to let him marry the Philistine girl. To celebrate the news, Samson threw a party for the bride and her friends and family. The bride's father sent over thirty young men from Timnah to keep Samson company and help prepare for his wedding.

Samson decided to tease the Philistine men and give them a challenge they could never win. "Let me ask you a riddle," he said. If the thirty men could solve the riddle within seven days, he would give them each a new set of clothes. If they could not, they each had to give him the same.

Here is the riddle:

"OUT OF THE ONE WHO EATS CAME SOMETHING TO EAT; OUT OF THE STRONG ONE CAME SOMETHING SWEET."

Of course, you know what the answer was: the lion! But no one else knew that

Samson had killed a man-eating lion that then became home to a beehive filled with honey. The men could not guess the answer, but they did not want to give Samson a reward. They went to Samson's bride and threatened to kill her and her family if she didn't find out the answer and tell them.

Samson's bride didn't know the answer. She didn't want to trick Samson, but she had to protect her family. So she went to Samson and begged him to confide in her. "You hate me!" she cried. "You don't really love me. You have given my people a riddle but you haven't told me the answer."

At first, Samson kept his silence for four days. But the woman cried and asked him again and again to tell her the answer. On the final day, he gave in with the answer. Of course, his bride went straight to the men and explained the riddle to save herself and her family. When the men answered correctly, Samson grew angry. He knew they could not

SAMSON'S BRIDE GAVE AWAY THE ANSWER.

have guessed the truth. He knew that the woman had betrayed his trust.

Samson did not want to pay a debt that the men earned by cheating, but he knew he owed them their reward. Then the Spirit of the Lord once again filled Samson with power. He went to a neighboring Philistine village, where he defeated thirty men with his bare hands and stole their clothes to give to the men as payment. Still angry with the young woman he was engaged to, he went home to calm down.

After he cooled down, he returned to her house to talk about their marriage, but when he arrived, he got another surprise. While he was away, she had married one of the men who had tricked him!

Well, as you can imagine, Samson was very angry. He went to her father to ask why he had been betrayed again. Her father

answered, "I thought you hated her!" He offered Samson his younger daughter as a bride instead, but that just made Samson even angrier. He was so angry, in fact, that he again ran off in a rage.

With his anger fueling his strength, he wanted to get revenge on the thirty men who not only had tricked him into losing the bet but had also stolen his bride. Samson went into the woods, captured three hundred foxes, tied torches to their tails, and set them loose in the crop fields of Timnah. The foxes spread fire wherever they ran, destroying the Philistines' food supply.

The Philistines knew that Samson was to blame for the destruction. They told the Israelites they must bring Samson to them to be judged. The Israelite men pleaded with Samson to turn himself in so their people could be saved. Samson agreed. He let his people bind him with ropes

SAMSON WAS STRONGER THAN A THOUSAND MEN!

and lead him to the Philistines to be judged.

As his people turned Samson over to his enemies, again the Spirit of the Lord gave him great power. Samson flexed his strong muscles and snapped the sturdy ropes as if they were thread! Free from his bonds, he grabbed a donkey's bone from the ground and swung it over his head. He swung the bone again and again, defeating a thousand Philistines at once in the name of God and the Israelites!

The Philistines were defeated, just as the angel had promised. For the next twenty years, Samson ruled Israel in peace. In those years, you would think that Samson learned to hold his quick anger and use his strength more wisely.

Well, Samson was a kind and strong leader, but after all those years he never truly learned to trust God in hard situations. Instead, he let his emotions get out of control. Even superheroes as strong as Samson have weaknesses. The truly amazing part of the story: God found a way to use even Samson's weakness as part of His plan to free the people of Israel.

Where in the Bible?

You can read all about Sampson in Judges 13–16 and Hebrews 11:32. Some of the highlights:

- Samson is born with a special mission from God: Judges 13.
- Samson stops a lion with his bare hands: Judges 14:5–6.
- Samson overcomes a thousand men: Judges 14–15
- Samson is a hero of faith: Hebrews 11:32

Pray to Be . . . Super-Strong for God

Samson made some bad choices by putting himself in tough situations and letting his anger get the best of him. But God still was able to use him as part of His plan. Samson was physically strong, but what makes him a real superhero of faith is that he recognized that all his power came from God.

- Thank God for always being by your side to make you stronger.
- Pray to use God's power for His purposes, not with greed or revenge.
- Listen to God's plan for you.

THE STORY OF DAVID

After the people of Israel entered the Promised Land, there came a time when they wanted a king. They didn't need a king, because they had God to guide them. But the people still wanted a human king to lead them.

So God gave them a king named Saul. At first he was a good king, but he stopped listening to God. It was time for a king who loved God with all his heart and could teach the people to do the same.

God sent a messenger named Samuel to Bethlehem to find the king God had in mind. (Samuel was a prophet, which meant he knew God's will and was called to share it with the people.) The king was to be found at the house of a man named Jesse.

Now, Jesse had seven sons known for their strength. So Jesse called the first, thinking he surely had to be the king God had in mind. But Samuel said no, he was not the king God wanted. As each strong son came before Samuel, each was announced as "not the one."

Jesse and his sons were confused. Could Samuel be wrong? But Samuel knew God had a plan. He asked Jesse, "Are these *all* your sons?"

DAVID WAS YOUNG WHEN HE WAS CHOSEN BY GOD TO BE A KING.

DAVID WAS BRAVE IN PROTECTING THE SHEEP.

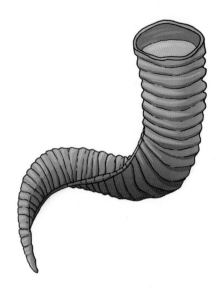

Though small, David was handsome. God spoke to Samuel, "*He* is the one." David was chosen. Samuel brought out the special ram's horn full of oil he had saved for the occasion. Samuel then anointed David's head, signaling God's choice that David would one day become king.

After he was chosen, David went back to work in the fields. Being a shepherd wasn't easy work. David learned to be brave to protect the sheep from wild animals. Only the bravest would take on a lion. But David killed a lion and a bear to keep his sheep safe. He grew stronger and gave his all as a shepherd, waiting for the time when he would be summoned to be king.

After a time, his eldest brothers went to serve in King

Jesse admitted that he had one more son, David—the youngest—who was out taking care of the sheep. Jesse was certain that if his other sons hadn't passed Samuel's judgment, David certainly wouldn't be a good candidate either. But Jesse obeyed and had David brought home to meet Samuel.

DAVID GAVE HIS ALL AS A SHEPHERD AND WAITED TO BE SUMMONED TO BE KING.

DAVID WOULDN'T LET THE GIANT TALK BADLY ABOUT GOD.

Saul's army. They were strong and a big help in the fight against the Philistine enemies. One day, Jesse sent David to bring bread to his brothers and find out how they were doing in battle. When he arrived at the battlefield, he saw that the Israelites were sorely outclassed. The Philistines had real giants on their side!

One of the giants was named Goliath. He was over nine feet tall, and his body was covered in armor. David learned that Goliath had been coming to the front lines every day for forty days, teasing the Israelites, "I dare you to choose one of your men to fight me. If he kills me, we will be your slaves. But if I kill him, you will be our slaves."

None of the Israelites dared go up against Goliath. But David spoke up about how bothered he was that Goliath would mock the Israelites and God. He knew he had God on his side and wanted to fight on the side of what was good.

David's words got back to King Saul, and the king sent for him. David immediately offered to fight the Philistines. King Saul took one look at the young shepherd and shook his head.

"How can a boy like you hope to defeat a trained warrior like Goliath?" asked King Saul. All David needed to do was remind Saul of how he had already killed both a lion and a bear to defend his sheep. He had the strength of God behind him.

Saul then looked more closely at David. He saw that David had an inner fire and strength like he had never seen before. King Saul gave David permission to

DAVID HAD ALREADY KILLED BOTH A LION AND A BEAR!

DAVID DEFEATED A GIANT WITH ONE STONE!

volunteer. He tried to give David his tunic and armor as well, but David refused.

On the way back to the battlefield, David grabbed five smooth stones from the riverbed and checked his slingshot to make sure it was in good working order. He then approached Goliath.

The giant towered in front of him. He looked down at young David and became angry that the Israelites would send such a joke to fight him. "I'll feed your body to the birds and the animals!" Goliath taunted David.

But David stood firm and called upon God. He placed one stone in his slingshot and flung it with all his might at the giant. The stone hit the giant right between the eyes, striking him dead instantly. The giant fell. The Israelites cheered, while the Philistines all fled in fear.

Where in the Bible?

You can read about David in 1 Samuel, 2 Samuel, and 1 Kings. Some of the highlights:

- David is chosen to be king: 1 Samuel 16:1–13

- David battles Goliath: 1 Samuel 17

Pray to Be . . . Super-Brave for God

From what we read in the Bible, David clearly didn't look like a king or a giant slayer. But that fact made him even more useful for God. David would need to depend on God's superpowers, not his own human power, to do big things.

- Thank God for the ways He can help us handle big problems.

- Pray to God to help you see what He sees in other people.

- Listen to God when He's asking you to stand up for what's right.

The Story of Elijah

THIS PROPHET BROUGHT ABOUT AMAZING MIRACLES FROM GOD THROUGH RAIN, BREAD, AND FIRE.

Back in the days of the Bible, it wasn't uncommon for people to worship many gods. There was a god of weather, a god of war, a god of death . . . you get the idea. People built altars and made sacrifices to these gods. Sometimes these people behaved very badly because they said the gods told them that was how they must behave.

KING AHAB AND QUEEN JEZEBEL WERE CRUEL TO THE ISRAELITES.

It was during this time that evil King Ahab and his wife Jezebel ruled Israel. They worshipped a god named Baal whom they said was the god of weather, and they killed many Israelites in the name of their false god.

Fortunately, Elijah was a prophet and he knew that the one true God was in charge of the weather. He went to King Ahab and Queen Jezebel and told them to behave well or he would ask God to stop all rain from falling in the land.

King Ahab laughed at Elijah. The king was confident that with Baal on his side, the rain would continue to fall, but he would soon find out that was very wrong.

For three years, no rain fell on the land. Animals were starving. Crops were drying up. No matter how hard the king and his wife prayed to their god, no rain fell.

GOD PROVIDED FOOD FOR ELIJAH.

Meanwhile, Elijah had escaped to an area where there was a spring with water to drink. A raven—a strong, black bird sent from the Lord—brought him bread and meat every day. Eventually, the spring dried up. When there was nothing left to drink, Elijah set out from his hiding place.

He did not have to go far before he came to the home of a woman and her son. They, too, had almost run out of food and water. All the woman had left was enough flour and oil to make one loaf of bread. She was saving it for one last meal for her son and herself.

But Elijah knew God's power was with him. He told the woman to bake a small loaf of bread and give it to him. If she did, he would make sure she would never run out of food and drink again.

The woman wasn't sure if she believed Elijah's promise, but she had nothing to lose. One loaf of bread wasn't enough to save their lives; after the bread was gone, they would soon starve. She poured flour and oil into the bowl to make the dough, and when she did, she was completely shocked. The containers of flour and oil were still full! Elijah had fulfilled his promise and made sure the woman and her son would never go hungry again.

The woman and her son were well fed, but later her son became sick. There was no cure for him and, sadly, he died. The woman went to Elijah and begged him for his help.

Once again Elijah felt the power of God within him. He went to the boy and spread his hands over him. He called out, "Oh Lord, let this boy live again!"

And just like that, the boy opened his eyes. He was alive and well! The woman now knew Elijah was truly sent from God to speak the truth.

GOD USED ELIJAH TO BRING A CHILD BACK TO LIFE.

Back at the kingdom of Ahab and Jezebel, there was more trouble brewing. Jezebel was so angry at Elijah for taking away their rain that she rounded up all of the Israelite prophets and ordered to have them killed.

Fortunately, not everyone in the land was so evil. Instead of killing the prophets, a servant named Obadiah was hiding them from the queen! Thanks to Obadiah, more than a hundred people's lives were spared.

Elijah was angry with the king and queen, and he grew tired of waiting for King Ahab to turn away from worshipping Baal. He wanted the king to stop ordering his servants to kill innocent people. He went to the kingdom and asked to see Ahab.

Ahab let him in and asked, "Are you the one who has been making all this trouble for Israel?" Elijah replied, "No, Ahab, you are. It's your fault that there is a drought."

Elijah told Ahab that it was time to stop behaving badly. It was time for the king to take responsibility and care for his people properly.

During his visit, Elijah saw that many of Ahab's subjects had started to believe in Baal as well, and were turning away from being good people. He could no longer wait for the king to change his mind. It was time for action.

He called for all of the people in Israel to meet him at the top of a mountain. There would be a contest to decide once and for all who was most powerful, Baal or God.

Some people were very curious to see what would happen. Elijah was counting on his enemies to show up, eager to laugh in his face. But he knew he would have the last laugh and show them all the truth.

Once all of the people were gathered at the top of the mountain, Elijah cleared two

ELIJAH TOOK ACTION TO GET PEOPLE TO BELIEVE IN GOD!

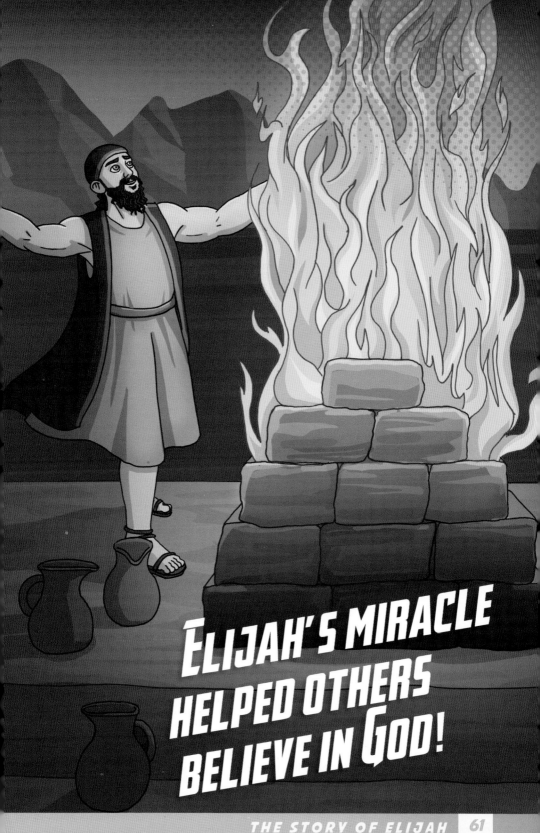

ELIJAH'S MIRACLE HELPED OTHERS BELIEVE IN GOD!

ELIJAH PRAYED TO GOD TO SHOW HIS POWER AND STRENGTH.

areas, one to be lit by Baal, and the other to be lit by God through Elijah. Whichever fire lit first would prove who was the true God. Everyone agreed this was a fair contest.

The worshippers of Baal went first. They prayed and danced from morning to night, but nothing stirred. Elijah laughed. "Shout louder!" he teased them. "Surely he is a god! Perhaps he is deep in thought, or busy, or traveling. Maybe he is sleeping and must be awakened!" So the priests shouted louder and tried even harder, but nothing happened.

Then it was Elijah's turn. He built a small pyramid of twelve stones and some wood. He then asked the people to pour twelve jugs of water onto his altar. The people laughed at him. Didn't he know that water was the enemy of fire? No fire could light on an altar drowned in water!

Elijah prayed to God to show His power and strength.

The altar caught fire, consuming the stones and the wood and drying up every last drop of the water! The fire blazed, lighting up the night. Everyone who witnessed this amazing feat believed Elijah's words and turned their hearts to God. As they did so, a strong rain finally began to fall, ending the drought and saving all the people of the land.

Elijah didn't rest after saving all of Israel from the evil king and queen. He went on to use his powers from God to part the river Jordan so his people could pass and call fire down from heaven to defeat his enemies.

Before he died, Elijah transferred the powers given to him by God to his companion Elisha so his good deeds could continue long after he was gone. Even Elijah's death was infused

ELIJAH WAS
CARRIED TO
HEAVEN IN A
CHARIOT OF FIRE.

RAIN FINALLY FELL AND SAVED THE PEOPLE!

with power. Instead of lying down and turning to dust when he died, he was taken up to heaven in a whirlwind pulled by a chariot and horses of fire.

Where in the Bible?

You can read about Elijah in 1 Kings and 2 Kings. Some of the highlights:

- Elijah gives endless flour and oil through God: 1 Kings 17:7–16

- Elijah brings a boy back to life through God: 1 Kings 17:17–24

- Elijah calls for fire on the mountain: 1 Kings 18:16–39

Pray to Be . . . Super-Powerful for God

Elijah was given a gift. He was a prophet, so he knew God in a special way. But he didn't use that gift for his own gain—he shared it with others to help them know God better, too.

- Thank God for the miracles He provides.

- Pray to God to do amazing things through you.

- Listen to God when He asks us to share His words with others.

THE STORY OF ESTHER

A YOUNG GIRL WON THE KING'S HEART AND SAVED THE LIVES OF HER PEOPLE.

Long ago, in Persia, there was a king named Xerxes. He was married to a beautiful woman named Queen Vashti, and he loved to show her off to his people. One day, he commanded her to make an appearance at a party to show everyone how pretty she was. Vashti refused and Xerxes was very angry.

ESTHER OBEYED AND WENT TO THE KING'S PALACE.

He asked some of his advisors what he should do. The decision: Banish Vashti and replace her as queen to show the people what would come of disobeying him. Xerxes followed this advice. With Vashti gone, he ordered a search throughout his entire kingdom to find a beautiful young bride to be his next queen.

Not far from his palace, his searchers discovered a woman named Esther, who was not only beautiful but kind and smart. She lived with her older cousin Mordecai, who had taken care of her ever since her parents died when she was young. They had been sent out of Israel and were living humble, quiet lives while hoping one day to return to their homeland. They kept their faith a secret as protection.

Esther probably did not want to go to the king's palace. She would be leaving her home,

ESTHER'S GOODNESS WON THE KING'S HEART, AND SHE BECAME QUEEN.

her friends, and her family. She may have heard how the king treated Vashti. She would not have wanted the king to find out about her people or their secret faith for fear they would be punished and even killed.

But as a young Jewish girl, Esther didn't have the right to say no to the king, so she went

HAMAN WAS EVIL AND HUNGRY FOR POWER!

off to meet the king. She kept her family background a secret, as Mordecai advised.

The moment they met, Xerxes was immediately drawn to Esther. He thought it was because of her outer beauty, but truly it was the goodness of her heart that shone through and won her the admiration of all who came to know her.

Soon, King Xerxes and Queen Esther were married. As they got to know each other better, the king saw how smart Esther was, and he began to turn to her as an advisor. Esther urged the king to be a kind ruler and helped her people whenever she could.

Unfortunately, the king also trusted the evil Haman, whom he had rewarded with a very high position as prime minister in his kingdom. Haman had the power to give orders—and he used them cruelly. He even made his subjects bow down to him.

Mordecai and his followers would not bow down to Haman, however. It was against their religion to bow down to anyone except God. Haman was so angry that he went to his friend the king. He told King Xerxes

that certain people were not obeying the king's laws and asked him to place a decree that said that anyone who disobeyed would be killed.

The king trusted his advisor, so without a second thought, he agreed. When Mordecai found out about this decree, he sent a secret message to his number-one spy in the castle, Queen Esther herself!

Esther was afraid, but she knew it was up to her to save her people. She asked her people to pray as she hatched a plan to help save the Jewish people and punish Haman at the same time.

Esther knew that the law said that if she approached the king without being asked, she would be killed, unless the king decided he wanted to see her. The sign of her acceptance from the king would be lowering the gold scepter toward her, which would mean she could live. She was scared, but the lives of all her people were at stake. So she put on her royal robe and went to the king's inner chambers. To her relief, he extended his gold scepter! Feeling bolder, Esther asked the king if he and Haman would join her the following evening at a banquet. Haman was pleased to be asked to dine with the king and queen. In the meantime, he ordered his men to build a gallows where Mordecai and all his followers would be hanged the very next day. This way, he could enjoy the evening's banquet, satisfied with knowing he had punished all those who had disrespected him.

That same night, God was working behind the scenes. The king couldn't sleep. He asked for a history book to be read to him. In the book was the record of a time not long past when a loyal subject—Mordecai—had foiled a plot to kill the king. The king remembered it and asked his servants what had been done to reward the man who had foiled the plot. "Nothing," they answered.

Xerxes immediately called Haman to his side. Haman was overjoyed! To be asked to dine with the king at a private banquet was an honor, but to be called to a private conference made Haman swell with pride. He swaggered into the king's chambers, ready to receive any reward the king wanted to hand him.

REWARDS FOR SAVING THE KING: A HORSE OF THE KING'S OWN AND A ROYAL ROBE.

"What should be done for the man the king delights to honor?" the king asked Haman. Haman couldn't believe his ears! He would get to choose his own reward!

He thought carefully, and gave his answer. "For the man the king delights to honor, have them bring a royal robe the king has worn and a horse the king has ridden, one with a royal crest placed on its head. Then let the robe and horse be entrusted to one of the king's most noble princes. Let them robe the man the king delights to honor and lead him on the horse through the city streets, proclaiming before him, 'This is what is done for the man the king delights to honor!'"

ESTHER SPOKE UP BOLDLY TO HELP HER PEOPLE.

The king clapped his hands with delight. He would do just what Haman had said. The king commanded Haman, "Go now. Get the robe and the horse and do just as you have suggested for Mordecai the Jew, who sits at the king's gate."

As soon as Haman left, he struggled to control his anger as he went to carry out the king's orders. Not only had Haman not received his cleverly crafted reward, but he had to give it to Mordecai, the man who would not bow down to him.

Haman went to the gate and brought Mordecai the reward. He led the royal horse through the city streets as Mordecai sat on top with honor and pride for saving the life of their king. Esther watched with great faith in what was to come—the prayers of her people were working. But the next step depended upon Esther's boldness alone.

That night at the banquet, Esther gathered her courage and spoke up. She revealed the secret about her faith and her family to the king. She told Xerxes that Mordecai was her beloved cousin and she begged him to spare her people.

The king had grown to love Esther and was disturbed that someone would want to hurt her and her people. While the king was still taking in this huge piece of news, the last piece of God's plan fell into place. One of Xerxes' attendants came forward and told the king about the gallows Haman had created

ESTHER WATCHED WITH GREAT FAITH IN WHAT WAS TO COME.

to secretly hang Mordecai the hero.

The king was furious! He ordered that Haman himself be taken away and hanged immediately for disrespecting the hero who had saved his life, as well as the life of his wife and all of her people. From that moment on, the king vowed to treat Mordecai and his people well. In every city, there was joy among the Jewish people. They celebrated Queen Esther for her courage.

Where in the Bible?

You can read about Esther in the book of Esther. Some of the highlights:

- Esther listens to Mordechai: Esther 4

- Esther begins a plan: Esther 5

- Esther tells Xerxes about the threat to her life and her people: Esther 7

Pray to Be . . . Super-Useful for God

Esther would never have expected to wind up as queen, but she used the chance to help others in a way only she could.

- Thank God for the places He sends you to be a blessing to others.

- Pray to God to see chances to make a difference.

- Listen to God when He nudges you to take action.

The Story of Paul

ANYONE, EVEN A BAD GUY, CAN CHANGE AND BE USED BY GOD.

A long time ago, a man named Saul did some really bad things. He led attacks on Christians. He had them chased out of their homes and villages and put them in prison. He ran through the streets with a sharp sword, calling out every Christian in the village to leave or be punished.

God saw this—because God sees everything—and He was angry. But God wasn't about to give up on Saul. Even though Saul was not tall and didn't have big muscles, God saw that Saul was strong on the inside. He was a leader. People listened to him, and he was a passionate man.

Most people wouldn't choose an enemy like Saul to lead their team, but God's ways are different than people's ways. God saw in Saul an opportunity to display His own grace and power. He had a plan.

One day, like any other day, Saul was on his way to carry out his evil deeds. He was traveling alone on the road to Damascus when a bright light appeared in front of him. It was shining down through the clouds. The light was so bright it blinded him!

Then a voice boomed down from the heavens above. The voice said, "Saul, Saul, why are you persecuting me?"

Saul knew it was the voice of Jesus, and he grew afraid. He bowed down before the light and trembled. He knew if God had singled him out to scold him, he must be in pretty big trouble! Jesus told Saul to go into the city and wait there to find out the next part of God's plan. When the light faded, Saul still couldn't see.

He made his way to the city, blind and afraid, and waited,

ANANIAS HEALED PAUL.

At that moment, Saul knew what he must do. He realized that Jesus had met him on that road to change Saul forever, and then sent Ananias to give him a new way of looking at life. Saul understood that Jesus had died on the cross to wipe out everyone's sins and that he had been forgiven for the terrible things he had done to Jesus's followers.

Saul thought that if he could be reborn as a new person with new sight, others could be, too. In the moment his sight was restored, Saul realized that God chose him of all the people in the world because God loved him and knew that he could change! And if God could do that for Saul, then Saul certainly had faith in God!

From that moment on, Saul was filled with the power of faith and goodness. And like any good superhero, he decided that a new name was in order. He would be Saul no longer. From that moment on, his name would be Paul. He would take his new role as an Apostle, and as a superhero fighting on the side of the Lord, to spread the

just like Jesus had instructed. After three days of stumbling blindly in the dark, Saul heard a knock at his door. It was a man named Ananias. Saul knew that Ananias was a devout follower of Jesus, and he thought Ananias had come to punish him even more. Instead of trying to run away, Saul met with Ananias, ready to pay for his crimes against God.

Ananias surprised Saul. He was not there to hurt him; he was there to heal him. He placed his hands on Saul and, just as suddenly as sight had been taken from him, his vision was restored. Saul could see again!

GOD SPOKE TO SAUL.

Word of Jesus Christ across the land.

Paul wandered from Jerusalem all the way to Rome, telling everyone he saw that Jesus had risen and was the true Son of God. Life wasn't easy for an Apostle, because in many places, Christianity was against the law. Anyone who was caught spreading the word of God would be arrested and badly hurt.

Paul was treated the same way he had treated other Christians before. He was placed in prison and watched by guards. Still he had faith, and that faith became his superpower.

At that time, Rome was one of the biggest, most powerful cities in all the land. Filled with courage, Paul decided to ask the Emperor of Rome to protect him as he spread the word of God across the land.

The Emperor was impressed. He wanted to meet this man who dared make such a bold request. But the Emperor was cautious, too. He sent a ship of armed guards to fetch Paul and bring him to Rome so he

PAUL SURVIVED A DANGEROUS STORM.

could meet this passionate and courageous man.

While they were at sea, Paul sensed a dangerous storm was rising up. He warned his guards, but they did not believe him. Soon, the sky grew dark and, as Paul predicted, a great storm suddenly rose up. The ship was wrecked and everyone on board was carried to an island. The people were safe, but the boat was ruined.

They were greeted by the native people of the island, who gave them food and drink and a place to sleep. Paul wanted to help. He gathered sticks to build

PRISON COULDN'T CONTAIN PAUL'S POWER AND FAITH IN GOD!

a fire. When he threw the wood onto the fire, a venomous snake that had been sleeping among the sticks leapt from the fire and bit Paul on the arm.

The men watched carefully, thinking that Paul was being punished and would die from the snakebite. But no harm came to Paul at all. When the guards saw that Paul wasn't affected by the bite, they believed he was filled with a special power that protected him. Paul told them that his power came from faith in God.

GOD PROTECTED PAUL FROM A POISONOUS SNAKE!

After three months of living on the island and listening to Paul preach the word of God, they were finally able to sail off to Rome as planned. Paul had gained the respect of the Roman guards, and he was allowed to live on his own as a teacher, spreading the word of God.

Paul met with many people. Some of them were sick or hurt and had given up hope. They needed healing for their bodies as well as their souls. One man Paul met had a lame leg and had never walked. At Paul's word, the man was healed through God's power. The man jumped up and began to walk. Paul healed many people's bodies and spirits with the power given him from God.

Although Paul performed miracles and was gentle and kind, he remained under guard for the rest of his days. The Romans were afraid of his power. But Paul's days of violence and anger were over now that his power came from God.

He spent the rest of his days spreading the word of God. The new, quiet power of his speech

THE WORD OF GOD SPREAD FAR THROUGH PAUL!

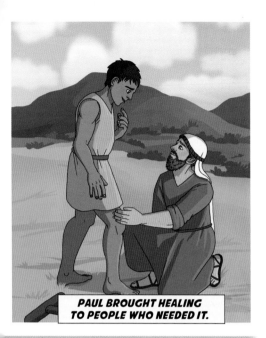

PAUL BROUGHT HEALING TO PEOPLE WHO NEEDED IT.

of God's greatest messengers on earth. His story is a reminder that anyone can change and be redeemed through God's grace and power.

Where in the Bible?

You can read about Paul in Acts, 1 Corinthians, 2 Corinthians, Galatians, and Philippians. Some of the highlights:

- Saul on the road to Damascus: Acts 9:1–9

- Paul heals a man's leg: Acts 14:8–10

- Paul is bitten by snake: Acts 28:1–6

and his belief was strong enough to convert many people to Christianity and turn their hearts toward good, away from evil.

God's mercy helped Saul change from being a big bully to being the Apostle Paul, one

Pray to Be . . . Super-Forgiving

God loves us in spite of our sin. God even loved Saul, who was once convinced he was right as he killed others. God asks us to look for ways to bring out the good in others.

- Thank God for the new chances He gives us each day.
- Pray to God for help in forgiving.
- Listen to God when He tells you to share His glory with others.

THE STORY OF PETER

THIS BELOVED DISCIPLE OF JESUS WASN'T PERFECT, BUT HE BECAME THE FIRST GREAT LEADER OF THE CHURCH.

Jesus was a good, kind, perfect man when he was on earth. He had many followers, but he also had a few close friends. He called them his disciples.

One of his closest friends was Peter. Jesus called him his Rock, and the two spent a lot of time together, talking about God and what it meant to live a life pleasing to God. But Peter wasn't always a good, strong rock. In fact, when they first met, Peter was actually just a rough fisherman named Simon.

When you meet someone for the first time, your first impression of them comes from what they look like and what they say. But Jesus, the greatest superhero of all, could see more than that. When he met someone for the first time, he not only saw who that person was at that moment; he could also see into their heart and could see who that person could become.

The day that our story began, Simon was getting ready to go fishing. Simon's brother Andrew brought Jesus to him and introduced them. He said, "Simon, this is Jesus. He is the true Messenger of God."

Simon liked Jesus instantly. He had never met such a kind, gentle, and generous soul in his life. Although they were so different from each other when they met, Jesus knew they would one day become very close friends. He invited Simon and his brother. "Come, follow me."

Another time, as some of the fishermen, including Simon, were bringing in empty boats, Jesus asked them to take him out in a boat. Jesus spoke to them about many things. His ideas were unlike any they had ever heard, and they felt good and strong and true.

At one point, Jesus asked them to stop the boat and throw out their fishing nets. The fishermen protested at first, saying they hadn't caught anything all night. But then they listened to Jesus, and they pulled up more fish than they had ever caught before. They caught so many fish that the boat began to sink! Truly this was a miracle! Simon said to Jesus, "I'm not worthy to be near you."

But Jesus smiled. He looked at Simon and he didn't just see the rough fisherman who often spoke without thinking. Jesus read his character and saw into his heart. He saw the good and bad things Simon had done in his life and he had a clear vision of the kind of man Simon could become.

Jesus turned to Simon and announced, "You are Simon, but you will be Peter."

Now, the name Peter means "rock," but Simon didn't feel much like a rock. He felt more like a quiet observer of life. His name, Simon, meant "listen," and he had been listening to the sea and the wind and the people around him his whole life.

Anyone who knew Simon thought of him as a simple man, and no one thought he would ever amount to anything special. But Jesus did, and that was enough for Simon. Jesus was challenging him to change his ways and become a rock—a solid man people could rely on, a strong leader. He liked the idea of making such a big change, and he felt in his heart that if he followed Jesus, he could become that person.

Peter didn't become a hero that first day. He listened—like he had done his whole life— and watched and learned from Jesus. He knew what an honor

PETER FOLLOWED JESUS AND PERFORMED AMAZING MIRACLES.

it was to be invited into Jesus's inner circle.

But he didn't follow Jesus blindly, and he didn't always accept his teachings as truth. He challenged Jesus's ideas. He tried things and failed. He often questioned Jesus's belief. But Jesus forgave Peter when he failed, and prayed when Peter questioned. Peter became stronger, and eventually he lived up to his new name.

Jesus continued to travel for some time with his disciples. After a long day of healing the sick and performing miracles, Jesus went up to the top of a mountain to pray.

You might think that the Son of God would not need to pray, but you would be wrong. Performing miracles and being strong for everyone can take a lot of effort, even for a Savior, and Jesus had to pray to his Father, God, for strength and renewal to be able to carry out His work on earth.

Jesus told his disciples not to wait for him, and that he would meet up with them after his

prayer. But it was late at night when Jesus came down from the mountain, and the boat had already gone. Jesus saw the boat in the middle of the water and decided to walk across the water to meet them!

When Peter and the other disciples saw Jesus walking across the deep water as if it were solid land, they were shocked and a little afraid. "If you really are Jesus, make me walk on water, too," Peter challenged. Jesus stretched out his hand and Peter cautiously stepped out onto the surface.

Peter couldn't believe it! He was really walking on water! But as soon as he took his eyes off Jesus, Peter began to fall into the water. Jesus reached out his hand and lifted Peter up to safety. This was the first miracle performed through Peter, but it certainly wasn't the last.

One day, while traveling near the Sea of Galilee, Jesus asked his twelve disciples what people thought of him. They admitted that people did not understand him. But Peter said, "You are the Christ, the Son of the living God." Jesus was happy to see that Peter was so sure. He told Peter that he was now ready to be the strong Rock on which his church would be built.

Jesus handed Peter a lot of responsibility that day, but Peter felt he was ready. As a friend to Jesus, he still challenged him and argued when he thought Jesus was making a mistake. When Jesus told his disciples that he would have to suffer and die as part of his mission, it was Peter who tried to keep him from the cross.

The idea of standing by when his teacher and best friend was going to suffer was too much for him to bear. But Jesus didn't want Peter to keep him from doing what he knew he had to do. Then Peter became afraid and said he didn't even know Jesus. When Peter realized how he had acted, he was filled with sadness and shame. He had disappointed Jesus and lost him on the same day.

When Jesus rose from the dead, the first disciple he appeared to was Peter. Jesus forgave his friend and told Peter that he was now the leader of his people, the Rock of the

GOD SENT AN ANGEL TO FREE PETER, HIS IMPORTANT ROCK!

PETER HEALED PEOPLE IN THE NAME OF JESUS.

church. Peter had been given the power to do God's work on earth. From that day forward, he traveled and preached the word of Christ to anyone who would listen, and more people began to listen to him with each passing day.

King Herod heard about Peter and he grew angry. The King was no friend to Christians and he had many of Christ's followers killed. He decided to have Peter thrown in jail to keep him from spreading the word of God, and set sixteen soldiers to guard his cell.

Peter's friends and followers prayed for Peter to be released, and God heard their prayers. He sent an angel to help Peter break free. The angel appeared in Peter's cell and led Peter out of the jail, right past all of the guards and through the locked door! Peter was once again free to travel and spread the word to fulfill his promise to Jesus.

It wasn't long before people began to come to Peter with their problems, and Peter tried to help as best he could. One day, near Jerusalem, he heard about a man named Aeneas who was so sick, he had been lying in bed for eight years.

Peter went to him in faith. "Aeneas, Jesus Christ makes you whole," he said. "Stand up and make your bed!" And to everyone's amazement, Aeneas stood up strong and tall. He was cured!

Word quickly spread across the land, and Peter was called upon to heal people and bless them in the name of Jesus. A short time after he healed Aeneas, two men came to find him. They were very upset. A kind and generous wealthy woman had died, and the whole town was grieving. They asked Peter to heal her.

Peter looked deep inside his heart just as Jesus used to do, and he believed that he could do it. He followed the men and saw the woman's body lying there. Filled with the power and spirit of his faith, he commanded her to rise up, and she did. The town rejoiced. The woman was once again alive and able to perform all of her charitable works for her friends and neighbors.

Word continued to spread even farther of Peter's deeds

PETER SPREAD GOD'S LOVE, POWER, AND MESSAGE WHEREVER HE COULD.

Where in the Bible?

You can read about Peter in Matthew, Mark, Luke, John, and Acts. Some of the highlights:

- Simon witnesses the miracle of the fish: Luke 5:1–11

- Peter walks on water: Matthew 14:22–33

- An angel leads Peter out of jail: Acts 12:1–18

- Peter raises a woman from the dead: Acts 9:36–42

and of his faith in Jesus Christ. He continued to help people wherever he went. His power was so strong that people even tried to pass under Peter's shadow for healing! Jesus's prophecy had been fulfilled. Simon the simple fisherman became Peter the Rock, the first leader of the Christian people.

Pray to Be . . .
Super-Changed for God

As you read Simon's story, it's hard to believe that he becomes the leader Peter. But Jesus has a way of changing lives.

- Thank God for the hero He sees in each of us.

- Pray to God to make you a leader for Him.

- Listen to God when He tells you you're good enough to do His work.

THE STORY OF MARY OF NAZARETH

Once there was a girl named Mary. She was poor and came from a humble town. When Mary was old enough, she was promised to marry a man named Joseph.

One day, not long before their wedding, Mary was sitting by herself in her parents' house. Suddenly, an angel appeared in front of her. At first she was afraid. But the angel was so gentle and kind, she listened and accepted what she heard. The angel told her that because she was obedient and faithful, God had chosen her to be the mother of a very special baby.

Now Mary was even more surprised: she wasn't married yet. But the angel reassured her that the Holy Spirit of God would perform a miracle to create this baby, and so he would become known as the Son of God. Mary grew very quiet. She was honored to have been chosen by God for such an important role.

"I will do whatever God needs me to do," Mary replied. The angel disappeared, leaving Mary alone to wonder at what she had seen and heard.

AN ANGEL BROUGHT A VERY SPECIAL MESSAGE TO MARY.

OUR SAVIOR JESUS WAS BORN IN A PLACE WHERE ANIMALS WERE KEPT.

When Joseph heard the news, however, he was very confused. He didn't want to marry Mary if she was having a baby that wasn't his child. But he didn't want others to look down on her if he made this decision. So he planned to go through with the marriage and then divorce her quietly.

All that changed when an angel came to him in a dream. The angel told Joseph that everything Mary had said was true—that this baby was a gift from God. The angel told Joseph to name the baby Jesus. Joseph believed and obeyed, and Mary and Joseph were soon married.

But the couple could not simply prepare for the baby Jesus to come. The Emperor ordered everyone to come to Bethlehem to be counted and registered. The trip was long and hard, over difficult roads. It was especially hard for Mary because she was pregnant, but she did not complain.

To make matters worse, when they finally arrived in Bethlehem, there was no place for them to stay and Mary was about to have her baby! They looked everywhere. Finally, someone took pity on the couple and let them stay in a barn.

The baby Jesus was born that night. Mary loved him and took care of him. She was the best mother she could be to her son all the days of her life. Mary supported Jesus in everything he did, encouraged his devotion to God, alerted him to danger, and was there for him whenever he needed her.

Under Mary's strict but loving guidance, Jesus grew up to be a very sensitive and thoughtful boy. She instructed him in religion and taught him to love God and serve Him well. Jesus found that he loved spending time in the synagogue, listening to the men talk about God and debate points of the religious law.

As a boy, Jesus already felt a powerful connection to God. His mother had taught him well, and he grew up to be a confident young man who had a strong sense of his place in the world.

He felt so at home in the temple that one day, a funny thing happened. Mary, Joseph, and Jesus were visiting Jerusalem with many other

JESUS TURNED WATER INTO WINE—A MIRACLE!

JESUS WAS LOST BUT FOUND IN THE TEMPLE.

them! They traveled all the way back to Jerusalem to find Jesus studying with the men in the House of God. He was surprised his parents hadn't realized that was where he would be. "After all," Jesus told them, "I am in the house of my Father."

Aside from that one occasion when he was lost in the temple, Mary kept a watchful eye on her son even as an adult. She guided and protected him when she needed to.

One time, Mary and Jesus attended a wedding. During the wedding, Mary saw that the wine had run out. Running out of wine would have been very embarrassing to the family hosting the wedding. Mary pointed it out to Jesus, signaling that he should do something about it. If it was in his power to lend a hand, he should help.

Without waiting for a reply, Mary turned to the servants and told them to obey whatever Jesus instructed them to do. In turn, Jesus obeyed his mother.

He instructed the servants to fill six large stone jars with water. When they poured out the water,

travelers to celebrate the Jewish holiday of Passover. In the Jewish religion, once a boy turns twelve, he goes from being a child and spending time in the care of the women to being a man and spending time among the men.

Jesus had just turned twelve and was feeling independent. When they packed up to leave, Mary thought Jesus was with Joseph and Joseph thought he was with Mary. When they arrived at home, they realized that Jesus wasn't with either of

MARY KNEW GOD HAD A PLAN FOR JESUS.

the servers were completely surprised to find that it had turned into wine! The family's reputation was saved and Jesus had performed his first true miracle, all thanks to Mary's gentle reminder to always help if it's in your power.

Mary often went with Jesus when he traveled around the country to spread his teaching. She saw how the people in charge mistrusted Jesus and were angry with him. She wanted to protect him, but she knew that she could not change his path. Sadly, the authorities caught Jesus and had him killed.

Mary felt such grief and pain that she stayed with him until he died on the cross. She loved and supported him to the end of his days on earth.

Where in the Bible?

You can read about Mary in Matthew, Luke, and John. Some of the highlights:

- An angel appears to Mary: Luke 1:26–38

- Mary's song to the Lord: Luke 1:46–55

- Mary asks Jesus to turn water into wine: John 2:1–5

- Mary stays with Jesus at the crucifixion: John 19:25–27

Pray to Be . . .
Super-Ready for God

Mary questioned *how* things were going to happen, but she never questioned *what* was going to happen. She accepted that she would give birth to Jesus, Son of God.

- Thank God for inviting us all to be part of His story.

- Pray to God to say "Yes" when He calls.

- Listen to God when He has a plan—no matter how strange it seems.

THE STORY OF JESUS

THE ULTIMATE SUPERHERO SHOWED US HIS AMAZIN LOVE AND POWER THROUGH EVERY ACT ON EARTH INCLUDING HIS DEATH AND RESURRECTION.

On the night Jesus was born, a new star appeared in the sky. Wise men from far away had been watching the skies for a sign that a new messenger would come to heal the world and make it a better place for everyone. The wise men saw the star in the sky and traveled to find the child.

From that moment forward, word spread of the miraculous birth of the child who would come to save them. Jesus grew up in his parents' home and was a good, obedient child. He studied hard and obeyed all of God's commandments. He resisted temptation and made good choices, even though that wasn't always easy to do.

As a grownup, Jesus traveled the land, teaching anyone who wanted to listen. He taught through telling stories, and because he was such a good storyteller, a lot of people wanted to listen to him!

His stories taught people that God was the one true king, and that people should love God and love each other. He taught people how to communicate with God through prayer and how to trust in God when they needed guidance or strength.

But Jesus wasn't just a good storyteller. Through his power, he was able to perform amazing miracles. Word spread of his power and the miracles he could perform. People who were not being treated well by the Roman Empire asked him to come and help him. But when he arrived, they were surprised that he did not bring an army or show any force.

Jesus arrived in simple robes, riding a slow little donkey to

JESUS USED STORIES TO TEACH PEOPLE ABOUT GOD.

show he came in peace. Instead of starting a war, he said that people should love their enemies.

Traveling so much could be a lonely business, but fortunately Jesus had twelve friends whom he really trusted. He called them his disciples, and they traveled everywhere with him. As Jesus traveled from place to place, wherever he saw suffering, he did what he could to help. When he met a blind man, he placed his hands on the man and suddenly he could see. When he met a man who couldn't walk, he healed the man with only his touch and the man was able to get up and walk home.

Word continued to spread about this miracle man who

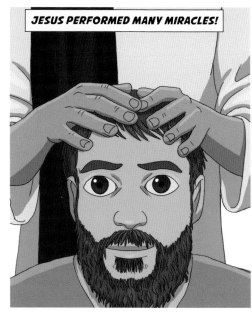

JESUS PERFORMED MANY MIRACLES!

had such power. Often when he arrived at a town, people already knew he was coming and had gathered to hear him speak. Being so famous wasn't easy for Jesus, but he didn't complain.

When his cousin and friend, John the Baptist, died, he just wanted to be alone. He rowed

JESUS USED HIS POWER TO HELP PEOPLE.

off in a boat to a remote place, but when he got to the other shore, he found that thousands of people had come to meet him. Jesus greeted them with love. He spoke and listened, and healed people who had come from far away. He did not stop until everyone had been taken care of, and by then it was very late.

The disciples suggested that he send the people away to local towns where they could get some food and a place to sleep, but no one wanted to leave his powerful presence. Jesus told his friends to feed the people instead.

His disciples went through their bags and collected all the food they had and looked at it. They shook their heads sadly. Among them, they only had five loaves of bread and two fish. That was barely enough to feed twelve disciples and Jesus himself, not to mention thousands of hungry travelers!

But Jesus looked at the food and knew it would be enough. He took the food, looked up to heaven, said a prayer of thanksgiving, and broke the loaves in half. He put the bread into baskets and asked his apostles to hand out the bread to the waiting people.

Each time the apostles reached into the baskets, there was food to hand out! By the time the baskets were empty, everyone had eaten. He had provided for each person in the crowd of more than five thousand people with only a few loaves of bread and two small fish. In fact, there were even leftovers!

Not everyone was happy with Jesus, however. Many people were corrupt and did bad things. When Jesus saw people cheating or not treating others

JESUS TOOK CARE OF PEOPLE'S NEEDS.

JESUS FED MORE THAN FIVE THOUSAND PEOPLE WITH ONLY A FEW LOAVES OF BREAD AND TWO FISH!

fairly, he would put a stop to it. He exposed powerful people who lied and took advantage of people to make themselves richer, and that made those people very angry.

These powerful people went to the Roman government and told the officers that Jesus was calling himself the king. Disrespecting the authority of Caesar and the Roman Empire was a crime. The Roman soldiers set out to find Jesus so they could arrest him, but his friends and followers would not turn him in.

One night, Jesus and his apostles gathered for a meal to celebrate the Jewish holiday of Passover. This holiday was to remember when the angel of death passed over the houses of their people to save them from the plague and set them free from slavery in Egypt.

As they celebrated together, only Jesus knew that it would be their last supper together. He told his disciples that he was granting them special powers, and that they would be able to perform miracles, too.

Jesus knew that one of his closest friends at the meal that night would betray him. He told the men gathered at the table, but they would not believe that any one of his best friends, who had been through so much with him, would turn him in to be killed by the Romans.

The soldiers offered thirty coins to the person who turned Jesus over to them. When the

JESUS IS OUR HERO AND THE HEALER OF OUR HEARTS!

JESUS KNEW THIS MEAL WOULD BE HIS LAST SUPPER WITH HIS DISCIPLES.

THE TOMB WAS EMPTY—JESUS HAD RISEN FROM THE DEAD!

JESUS WENT TO THE CROSS, ACCORDING TO GOD'S PLAN TO SAVE US ALL.

soldiers came for Jesus, it was his disciple Judas who turned him in for the reward. Jesus was sentenced to death like a common thief or murderer for his crime of going against the government.

Although some of his followers protested, Jesus was calm and took the sentence without complaint or struggle. He knew it was God's plan that he would take the punishment for all the wrong things people do. Jesus would take that sin on himself to heal all our hearts. He was the only one who could do it because he was the only perfect person who ever lived. How amazing is our biggest hero!

When Jesus died on the cross, his followers took down his body and placed it in a tomb. They placed a rock over the entrance to the tomb and sat outside to mourn his death. The morning after the Sabbath, some of the women went to the tomb to prepare his body for burial and were shocked to discover that Jesus's body was not there!

An angel appeared and told them that Jesus had risen from the dead and was on his way to Galilee. When the people found out about this big miracle, they traveled from near and far to Galilee to see for themselves this superhero who couldn't even be conquered by death.

Because of everything that had happened, Jesus's friends were afraid. They hid in an upper room with the door locked. But suddenly Jesus appeared and was standing there in the room with the disciples! Everyone looked up as though they had seen a ghost. They had seen him dead and buried in the cave, after all. But Jesus reassured them all. "Touch me and see," he said to them.

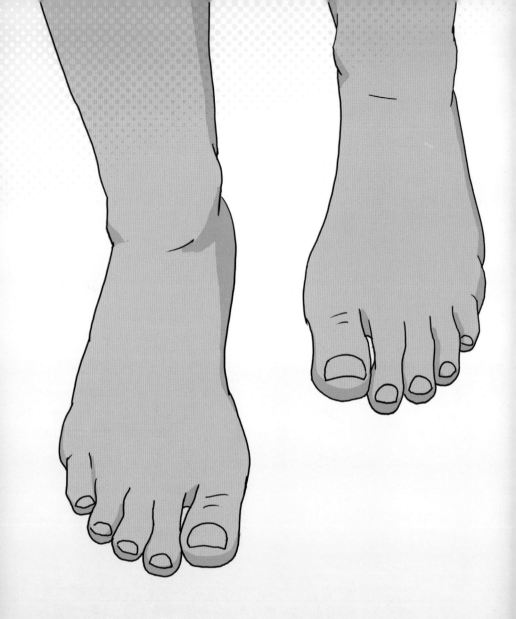

JESUS WENT HOME TO HEAVEN, BUT WE CONTINUE HIS WORK ON EARTH.

Jesus stayed on earth for forty days, performing miracles and giving his disciples instructions. It was their job to carry on his works and to share what they'd learned from Jesus with the rest of the world. They needed to write down what Jesus had told them and what they had seen in their travels with him, and tell people that Jesus was the savior that the Jewish people had been waiting for. Jesus wanted the disciples to tell everyone that He had come to experience God's punishment for sin, so that we don't have to. Jesus lived and died so that we can have a good relationship with God, the way Adam and Eve did before they disobeyed God and sin entered the world.

The disciples were called to perform superhuman feats like feeding hungry people, healing the sick, and raising people from the dead who still had work to do on earth. Most of all, they must tell everyone how much God and Jesus love them and how everyone can come home to God because of what Jesus did to rescue the world.

Once he was satisfied that all of his disciples knew what they needed to do, Jesus gathered them together one final time. He stood in front of them and bid them farewell.

JESUS COULDN'T EVEN BE CONQUERED BY DEATH!

Then his feet rose up off the ground and, as his disciples watched, he was taken up to heaven. Two shining messengers appeared, telling them that one day Jesus would come back to Earth in the same way he went to heaven.

Where in the Bible?

You can read about Jesus throughout the Bible, but especially in the New Testament books of Matthew, Mark, Luke, and John. Many of the stories appear in more than one book of the Bible. Some of the highlights:

- Jesus is born: Luke 2:1–20

- Jesus feeds more than five thousand: Matthew 14:13–21

- Jesus dies for our sins: Luke 23:32–48

- Jesus rises from the dead and ascends to heaven: Mark 16

Pray to Be . . . Super-Loving

Jesus is the best example we can follow. He is our ultimate superhero!

- Thank God for sending Jesus to love us and forgive our sins.

- Pray to God to follow Jesus's example.

- Listen to God when He shows us ways to follow Jesus.